The Voyageur in the Illinois Country

CENTER FOR FRENCH COLONIAL STUDIES
CENTRE POUR L'ETUDE DU PAYS DES ILLINOIS
WILLIAM L. POTTER PUBLICATION SERIES

THE CENTER FOR FRENCH COLONIAL STUDIES, INC.

WILLIAM L. POTTER PUBLICATION SERIES
(FORMERLY EXTENDED PUBLICATIONS SERIES)

SERIES EDITOR, BENN E. WILLIAMS

About the Center for French Colonial Studies (CFCS):

Founded in 1983, the Center for French Colonial Studies, also known as the Centre pour l'étude du pays des Illinois, promotes and encourages research into the social, political, and material history of the French colonies and French people of the Middle Mississippi Valley and the Midwest, with special focus on the Illinois Country in the seventeenth, eighteenth, and early nineteenth centuries. CFCS is organized as a 501(c)(3) corporation for exclusively charitable, literary, scientific and educational purposes. In now its third decade, the membership continues to consist of historians, archeologists, preservation technologists, architectural historians, genealogists, historic interpreters, and interested laypeople.

About CFCS's William L. Potter Publication Series:

The dissemination of knowledge forms an integral part of the organization's mission. One means to this end is the annual autumnal meeting and conference; another is the publication of the quarterly *Le Journal*, which emphasizes original research, book reviews, announcements, and news relating to the Center's mission. Recognizing a "publications gap" between shorter articles and monograph-length works, CFCS initiated its *Extended Publications Series* in order to make additional scholarship available to the public. This program publishes essays, monographs, and translations of primary documents that might not otherwise enjoy a place in print owing to their in-between length or esoteric nature. The name of the series was changed in 2011 to honor the memory of longtime series editor, board member, and past president William L. Potter.

Titles in the William L. Potter Publication Series

Jean-Baptiste Cardinal and the Affair of Gratiot's Boat: An Incident in the American Revolution
  Robert C. Wiederaenders

Louis Lorimier in the American Revolution, 1777-1782: A Mémoire by an Ohio Indian Trader
  and British Partisan
  Paul L. Stevens

Code Noir: The Colonial Slave Laws in French Mid-America [Bilingual edition]
  William Potter, editor; B. Pierre Lebeau, translator; and a preface by Carl J. Ekberg

French Colonial Studies: *Le Pays des Illinois*; Selections from *Le Journal*, 1983-2005
  Margaret K. Brown and H. Randolph Williams, editors

Plumbing the Depths of the Upper Mississippi Valley. Julien Dubuque, Native Americans, and Lead Mining
  With Annotated, Transcribed, and Translated Original Documents
  B. Pierre Lebeau; Lucy Eldersveld Murphy; Robert C. Wiederaenders

Standing Up for Indians. Baptism Registers as an Untapped Source for Multicultural Relations in St. Louis, 1766-1821
  Sharon Person

The Voyageur in the Illinois Country
The Fur Trade's Professional Boatmen in Mid America

Based on Unpublished Documents from the Kaskaskia Manuscript Collection and related sources.

Margaret Kimball Brown

CENTER FOR FRENCH COLONIAL STUDIES
CENTRE POUR L'ETUDE DU PAYS DES ILLINOIS
WILLIAM L. POTTER PUBLICATION SERIES
NUMBER 3

THE CENTER FOR FRENCH COLONIAL STUDIES, INC.
P. O. Box 482
St. Louis, MO 63006-0482
USA

ISBN: ISBN-13: 978-0615628523 ISBN-10:0615628524

Series editor: Benn E. Williams
Original cover design by William L. Potter; the new cover incorporates his illustration of an Illinois Country Pirogue ©2002 and used with the permission of his estate.

1. Fur trade - Mississippi River Valley - History - 18th century. 2. Fur traders - Mississippi River Valley - History - 18th century. 3. Fur trade - Illinois - History - 18th century. 4. Fur traders - Illinois - History - 18th century.
F352 .B76 2002

PREFACE

This is a reprint of the third installment in the *William L. Potter Publication Series*, formerly the *Extended Publications Series*, published by the Center for French Colonial Studies (CFCS). Founded in 1983, the CFCS is a non-profit organization devoted to raising and supporting public and scholarly interest in the historical French presence in the middle and upper portions of the Mississippi Valley, with special focus on the Illinois Country. The dissemination of knowledge forms an integral part of the organization's mission and we are able to do so in a variety of ways: notably via an annual autumnal conference (with invited speakers), the funding of the annual Carl J. Ekberg Research Grant, and the publication of the quarterly *Le Journal*, which presents original research, book reviews, announcements, and news. Recognizing a "publications gap" between shorter articles and monograph-length works, the CFCS initiated its *Extended Publications Series* in order to publish essays, monographs, translations of primary documents, etc., that may not otherwise enjoy a place in print owing to their in-between length or esoteric nature.

The series has been renamed to honor the memory of William L. Potter, its former editor and longtime board member and past president of the Center for French Colonial Studies. Bill set a high standard for the series and it is only fitting reprint a work that bears his fingerprints, from the clean design and introductory text (infra) to the illustrations. (We thank his family for allowing us to use his image of a *pirogue* for the cover.) The body of the manuscript is reprinted exactly, including the original dedication and cover page, albeit shrunk to fit into the series' current smaller format. To ease cataloguing, the copyright page now bears an International Standard Book Number (ISBN) and the subject keywords provided by the bibliographers at the University of Illinois at Chicago's Daley Library.

Benn E. Williams
Editor, William L. Potter Publication Series
Center for French Colonial Studies

About this work

The French voyageur cuts a dashing figure in our imaginations, so much so we often overlook the reality of his profession: it was a job. Margaret Brown looks at the business end of being a waterman in the remote French settlements of the Illinois Country in the mid-18th century; she presents her picture of the voyageurs' world from the perspective offered by the contracts, debts, and inventories they left behind. But there is still room for danger and adventure, to be sure: hunger, hardship, captivity, escape, and sudden death punctuate their workday-world.

This story of the Illinois Country voyageur is gleaned largely from an assemblage of some 7000 unsorted and mostly unpublished French documents and records known collectively as the Kaskaskia Manuscripts. Few people are as familiar with this collection as Dr. Brown, who (along with colleague Lawrie Cena Dean) has worked with this and other caches of French Illinois records for years (their calendar of the Kaskaskia Manuscripts is currently on microfilm and is pending publication, their compilation of documents from the community surrounding Fort de Chartres is scheduled for republishing soon).

The Voyageur in the Illinois Country expands our knowledge of other aspects of life in the French Midwest beyond the fur trade. Three complete inventories of household goods are presented and discussed. We learn a few things about the watercraft in use locally (*not* the romantic birch bark canoe, incidentally). We also learn that French/Indian relations were not always as cordial as popular history often paints them to have been. Above all, we see a little more of the voyageur than the swashbuckling canoe man of our imaginations.

About the Author

Margaret Brown received her Ph.D. in Anthropology from Michigan State University and is well known for her work in historic and prehistoric archeology. She retired as director of the famous Cahokia Mounds State Park archeological site and museum a few years ago. French Colonial Illinois has always been of particular interest to her, and that is reflected in some of the many titles she has published. She has authored (with colleague Lawrie Dean): *The Village of Chartres in Colonial Illinois, 1720-1765; The French Colony in the Mid-Mississippi Valley;* and the pending *Kaskaskia Manuscripts, 1714-1816.* Dr. Brown is the founder and first president of the Center for French Colonial Studies.

William L. Potter

THE VOYAGEUR
IN THE
ILLINOIS COUNTRY

THE FUR TRADE'S PROFESSIONAL
BOATMAN IN MID AMERICA

*Based on Unpublished Documents
from the Kaskaskia Manuscript Collection
and related sources.*

BY

MARGARET K. BROWN

CENTER FOR FRENCH COLONIAL STUDIES
EXTENDED PUBLICATIONS SERIES
NUMBER 3

PUBLISHED WITH PERMISSION BY
THE CENTER FOR FRENCH COLONIAL STUDIES, INC.
NAPERVILLE, ILLINOIS

In Memory of William Lemire

This volume in the Extended Publication Series is dedicated to the memory of William Lemire (1942-2002). A long time and dedicated supporter of the Center for French Colonial Studies/Centre pour l'étude du pays des Illinois, he served as its vice president during the last six years of his life. Of French Canadian origin, he enjoyed sharing his love for the study and preservation of the French heritage in North America.

CONTENTS

The Voyageur in the Illinois Country 1

Bibliography 29

Appendix

The Inventory of Antoine de Tonty 31

The Inventory of Francois Blot 33

The Inventory of Michel Le Cour 36

Maps

The Villages of the Illinois Country 3

North America--points relating to the text 11

Figures

Figure 1. Signature of Desruisseaux
 (sample page from Kaskaskia Manuscript).................. 4

Figure 2. An Illinois Country Pirogue 9

Figure 3. An 18th Century Batteau 9

Tables

Table 1. Destinations in Contracts 19

The Voyageur in the Illinois Country
by Margaret Kimball Brown

Voyageur-- the term brings to mind images of hardy men in birchbark canoes paddling the rivers out of Montreal and Quebec to trade with the Indians for furs. Indeed, the fur trade began in Canada, but as new areas were explored other centers of trade developed. The voyageurs were major contributors to the expansion of the French colonies in North America; as they moved west and south to find new sources for furs, they pushed the boundaries of known territories further and further out.

The beaver was the main impetus for the growth of the fur trade; its underfur made excellent felt for making fashionable men's hats in France. Areas south of the Great Lakes produced beaver fur less thick and dark than in the north, but the southern regions did hold other species whose hides were valuable-- particularly deer, buffalo and wildcat.

As the trade expanded geographically new bases were set up-- temporary wintering camps, fortified trading posts, and finally permanent villages. Far to the south of Canada below the junction of the Mississippi, Illinois, and Missouri rivers, a village developed upon a tributary river of the Mississippi. This village was settled by a segment of the Illinois Indians--the Kaskaskia--in 1703, and the river gained their name. Kaskaskia began as an Indian village with a few resident traders, but as the French population increased it grew into a major trade center.

This village and a few other small ones that formed in the area--Cahokia, Prairie du Rocher, St. Philippe, and the village surrounding the governmental center of Fort de Chartres-- were part of *le pays des Illinois*, the country of the Illinois, named for the Indian tribe. Initially the Illinois country was governed from New France (Canada). In 1717 the Illinois country became part of the colony of Louisiana. This colony stretched up the Mississippi river all the way from the Gulf of Mexico to the northern part of the present state of Illinois. The Illinois country included parts of what now are Missouri, Indiana, Iowa, and Ohio. The official (although loosely defined) boundaries of the Illinois country ran from about Peoria, Illinois, down to near the Arkansas post, east towards the Alleghenies, and west towards the Rockies.

Kaskaskia was a good location for trade; its site provided access to a vast river network: the Mississippi, the Missouri, the Ohio, the Wabash, the Illinois, and all their tributaries. Trade from Kaskaskia went north to Canada, Michilimackinac, and Detroit, and south down to all the posts on the Mississippi River, including New Orleans. By the 1730s, agricultural products grown in the productive Mississippi floodplain became major items in the southern trade, although trade also persisted with the Indians for hides and meat. Posts operating from the Illinois country were situated near the Ouia, Miami, Missouri and Osage Indians; in the late 1740s trade was carried on with the traditional enemies of the French, the Fox.

Merchants continued to trade down from Montreal, too, where they received official *congés* (permits) to trade in the Illinois. Traders prominent in the Kaskaskia records also appear on the Montreal *congés*: Grignon, Hamelin, Urtebrise, Le Duc, and others.[1] The number of official *congés* that were issued in New France varied over the years, but it was always less than the number of voyageurs who wanted to go on the fur trade circuit. Many of the traders were the illegal *coureurs-de-bois* (literally, "runners in the wood") who evaded the governmental restrictions. They were numerous, and the importance of their input into the fur trade based economy of Canada generally deterred official retaliation for their illegal actions.

Fort de Chartres was the center of the Illinois country government; very few governmental records have been preserved though, so little information exists concerning the issuing of *congés* from Fort de Chartres. A complaint from Canada indicates that Boisbriant (the first commandant at Fort de Chartres) did issue licenses to *coureurs-de-bois* from Canada.[2]

A glimpse at the life of a voyageur from Kaskaskia in the mid-eighteenth century can be gleaned from records preserved in the courthouse in Chester, Illinois, in a collection of documents known as the Kaskaskia Manuscripts. These documents came from the offices of the eighteenth century French notaries who drew up contracts-of-hire for voyageurs, partnerships between traders, notes of debts incurred in trade, and other agreements. The notaries' documents are records of the people-- the voyageurs, merchants, and farmers; the official government records were kept at Fort de Chartres. Not all of the notaries' records are preserved; during the years intervening from then to the present, loss has occurred. The majority of documents extant concerning voyageurs and traders comes from a ten year span: 1737-1748. A few are earlier, but virtually none are preserved from later years. This segment does give a good picture of the trade during the most prosperous period of the colony's life.[3]

The voyageur had to be an hardy individual, but the impression of voyageurs as uneducated, uncouth loners does not convey the true picture. Although the voyageurs were absent from their homes for long periods of time, they (like the rest of the colonists) valued family ties. Some married, had families in Kaskaskia or at Fort de Chartres, and owned land and cattle. Many maintained ties with their relatives in Canada. Very often when one member of a family moved to the Illinois from Canada others would follow. The settlers in Canada had intermarried, and this intermarriage continued in the Illinois, producing a network of relatives. Even marriages to Indians created networks, not only among the Indians, but also with Frenchmen married to other members of a tribe.

---

[1] John L. Morris, "The French Regime in Illinois" (Ph.D. diss., Urbana: University of Illinois, 1928),129ff.

[2] R. G. Thwaites, *The French Regime in Wisconsin*. in State Historical Society of Wisconsin, *Wisconsin Historical Collections* (Madison: State Historical Society of Wisconsin, 1908), 17: 438.

[3] Referenced documents from the Kaskaskia Manuscripts are calendared with English summaries. The originals have been photocopied and filed according to the calender number. The original documents are archived in temperature controlled storage. Copies can be examined in the Randolph County Clerk's office.

A few documents are quoted here in their entirety; most are summarized. Calendar summaries are by Lawrie Dean and where cited her translations are used. (See fn 6.)

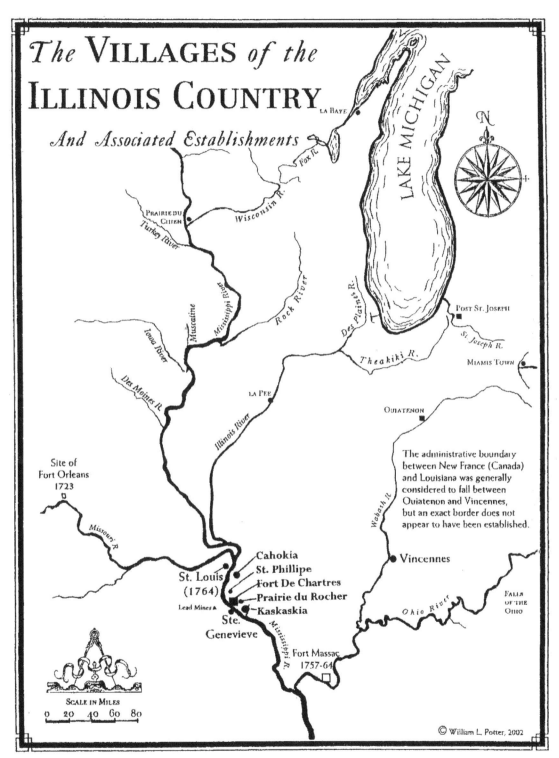

The Villages of the Illinois Country

And Associated Establishments

LA BAYE

LAKE MICHIGAN

Fox R.

N

PRAIRIE DU CHIEN

Turkey River

Wisconsin R.

Mississippi River

Muscatine

Iowa River

Rock River

Des Plaines R.

POST ST. JOSEPH

St. Joseph R.

MIAMIS TOWN

Theakiki R.

Des Moines R.

LA PEE

Illinois River

OUIATENON

The administrative boundary between New France (Canada) and Louisiana was generally considered to fall between Ouiatenon and Vincennes, but an exact border does not appear to have been established.

Site of Fort Orleans 1723

Missouri R.

Wabash R.

Vincennes

Cahokia
St. Phillipe
Fort De Chartres
Prairie du Rocher
Kaskaskia

St. Louis (1764)

Lead Mines

Ste. Genevieve

Mississippi R.

Fort Massac 1757-64

Ohio River

FALLS OF THE OHIO

© William L. Potter, 2002

SCALE IN MILES

0   20   40   60   80

Not all voyageurs were illiterate, some kept their own records of accounts; Michel Le Cour did, and the trader Desruissiaux signed his name on documents with a flourish. However, many voyageurs had to make their mark--an X--on their contracts. In such a case the contract was read aloud to them, and their mark made in agreement was verified by the royal notary and witnesses.

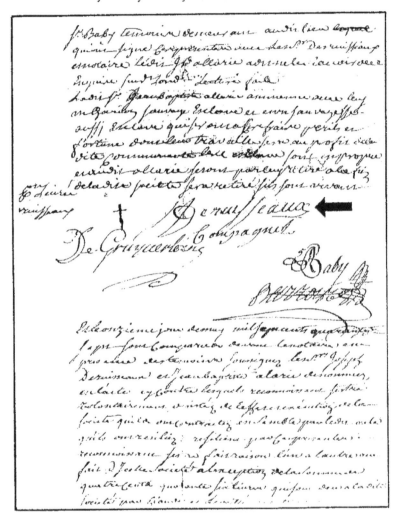

Figure 1. Signature of Desruisseaux. An example of a page from Randolph County, Illinois' *Kaskaskia Manuscripts*. [Kas. Mss. 45:6:28:2]

Despite the hardships of their life, the voyageurs participated in the local society. A later report speaking about the Frenchmen probably was pertinent for the 18th century as well:

> *And it is a remarkable fact, that the roughest hunter and boatman amongst them could at anytime appear in a ballroom, or other polite and gay assembly, with the carriage and behavior of a well-bred gentleman.*[4]

The inventories of the belongings of the voyageurs generally show at least a few good clothes suitable for dances. French women to dance with were hard to find though; there were always more men than women in the Illinois. By fourteen or fifteen years of age most French girls were married--to much older men. Widows generally remarried shortly after their husband's death. Marriages with Indian women were common, particularly in the early days of the colony. Much of the social life was for men only. Billiards was popular; the game was different from that of today, having both large and small balls. Each village had a couple billiard halls, rooms attached to homes. Evenings of drinking, gambling, and playing cards were popular.

The general term--voyageur--covered both those who held *congés* and the *coureurs-de-bois*. Although in general people think of the voyageur as paddling the canoe (and he did do that), being a voyageur from Kaskaskia could involve a variety of tasks: hunting, trapping, preparing pelts and meat for trade, carrying flour and other products to New Orleans for private traders or for the government, driving cattle long distances, and anything else that could be associated with trade.

Voyageurs were hired by an individual or by a partnership for paddling and other activities specified in a contract. These contracts were legal and binding on the parties. Several copies of the contract were made by the notary; one was given to each participant in the transaction and another was kept in the notary's file. The documents identify persons by various occupations--hunter, voyageur, trader, merchant--and also multiples of these: hunter/voyageur, voyageur/trader, trader/merchant. These designations appear to be fairly flexible depending on the time in a person's career the document was written, and also the tasks to be done.

Contracts for voyageur agreements followed a fairly standard format as can be seen from the following.

> *Before us, Billeron, royal notary in the province of the Illinois, in the presence of the undersigned witnesses was present Francois Pomil, currently in the Illinois, who by these presents has acknowledged that he has taken service with Sieur Jean Baptiste Denie to go to the sea and to help him hunt for the sum of 120 livres and 100 livres of meat and four pots[5] of oil which the said Sieur Denie will pay him at the sea as soon*

---

[4] Thomas Ford, *A History of Illinois from its commencement as a State in 1818 to 1847* (Ann Arbor, Michigan.: University Microfilms, 1968), 36.

[5] New Cassell's Dictionary (1967) states that a Canadian half gallon was a *pot* or *quarte*, equal to 63.4 ounces; see also: Paucton. *Métrologie ou Traité des Mesures, poids et monnoies...* (Paris: Chez La Veuve

as they arrive. The said Pomie undertakes to help unload the pirogue and to sell the meat. The said Pomie undertakes to serve the said Denie in everything that is possible and honest to do, to avoid losses and to warn him if someone intends him any harm. Promising and undertaking. Done and executed in our office in the presence of Sr. Tomas Chouin, witness, who has signed with us, this twenty-sixth of September, one thousand seven hundred and thirty-seven. The said Pomiey has declared he does not know how to sign this document, a reading having been made according to the ordinance.[6]

Before the notary at Fort de Chartres of the Illinois and the witnesses undersigned was present in person Charle Eslie, living at Fort de Chartres, who by these presents declares to contract with Sieur Charle Neau, Lieutenant of the militia of Fort de Chartres, to go on a voyage to the sea from Fort de Chartres to New Orleans and back. During which time and extent of the said voyage the said Charle Eslie promises and is obliged to work in the service and for the profit of the said Charle Neau in all things just and reasonable on the water in the bateaux, pirogues and on land. To do all that he is able and whatsoever is proper, to help carry and stow all goods before leaving the places and for the work of the voyage. The Sieur Charle Neau promises and obligates himself to pay and give as wages to Charle Eslie 200 livres in current money in paper or cards at New Orleans and he can purchase what he is able to from this in addition to a hat, two trade shirts, and a pair of ordinary stockings. Neau will permit the said Charle Eslie to transport in his boat when Sieur Neau goes back up to the Illinois a pot of brandy which will be counted and deducted from his wages and the rest of the merchandise. . . .[7]

When contracts were made with minors--that is, under twenty-five years--the young man's father had to agree to the contract:

Before the notary of Fort de Chartres and the undersigned witnesses was present Jean Baptiste Neport residing at Fort de Chartres, who has declared that he has taken service with Antoine Lesperance and Jean Baptiste Duplanty, partners, with the consent and permission of the Sieur Pierre Neport, his father, to help the said partners in their hunt along the rivers flowing into the Wabash during the course of this autumn and winter, to make with the said partners the voyage to New Orleans and to return with them to the Illinois, to work in their service at everything both necessary and reasonable, both for the said hunt and during the period of the said voyage which shall be over during the year 1738 when the said partners shall return to the Illinois with the convoy which shall arrive after their business at the sea is concluded. The

Desaint, Libraire, 1780).

[6]Lawrie Cena Dean and Margaret K. Brown, *The Kaskaskia Manuscripts 1714-1816: A Calendar of Civil Documents in Colonial Illinois* [Cited hereafter as Kas. Mss.] (Randolph County, Illinois: 1981) microfilm, 37:9:26:1, trans. by Lawrie Dean.

[7]Kas. Mss. 38:3:21:1, trans. by Lawrie Dean.

worker shall be fed during the said time. For this the said Antoine Lesperance and Jean Baptiste Duplanty, partners, promise and undertake jointly to pay and give to the said Jean Baptiste Neport 250 livres at New Orleans at port prices in cash or in merchandise and upon which sum the said partners shall give him twenty-five pots of brandy, good and sound, and shall allow him to load the said product of his wages in the craft which the said partners shall bring back to the Illinois granting him the costs of transport in their craft...[8]

Another youth was Pierrot Henrion, fourteen years old. His parents, Jean Henrion and Marie Barbe, contracted with Pierre Messager to have Pierrot work for him for three years for a wage of 300 livres; the money was to be paid to the parents. Pierrot was to receive his food, maintenance, and also religious instruction.[9]

Voyageurs and traders were not only the Canadian men usually depicted; free blacks, Indians, and women also took part in trade. Jacque Duverger, a free black, was not only a voyageur but also was referred to as a master surgeon. Andre Deguire *dit*[10] La Rose acknowledged a debt to Duverger for medicines and the care he had received from Duverger's wife during his illness. On the same day as the above document, Duverger made a partnership agreement with Pierre Doza to go and hunt meat to take to New Orleans. Doza was to supply three minots[11] of salt for salting the meat, and his son Joseph was to serve as a helper. Duverger was accompanied by his brother-in-law and Jean Baptiste Neport, the same fellow mentioned in a voyageur contract above. Neport was to receive 350 livres in coin or paper money, his food for the trip, and portage of 50 *pots* of brandy on the return trip.

Later, Duverger acquired 150 *pots* of bear oil, and he made an agreement with another voyageur, Joseph La Voix, to transport his bear oil to New Orleans, and for them to share equally in the profit from its sale. Duverger agreed to feed the man going in Doza's pirogue; in return for this he could use for his own trade goods whatever cargo space remained in the boat after Doza's goods were loaded for the trip back to Kaskaskia. Duverger died in 1743 and Bienvenu, a merchant/trader, was appointed as administrator of his estate.[12]

A number of women made agreements and took care of business while their husbands were away on trips. Dechofour de Louvier acknowledged a debt of 46 livres 40 sols to Madame Chevalier for goods; he promised to pay her in beaver or other furs. While Louis Metivier was away on a voyage his wife, Marie Faffard, was taken to court about a debt Metivier owed. Because the marriage was a community of goods it was a mutual debt and Marie was expected to pay it herself before Louis returned. At least one widow, Marie Genevieve Baudien, widow of Lefevre, took matters into

---

[8]Kas. Mss. 371011, trans by Lawrie Dean.

[9]Kas. Mss. 41:1:18:1.

[10]Dit" will not be translated. It has the meaning of "called", "known as"; it may be a nickname, but also may refer to a family name or "place of origin."

[11]A dry measure equal to about 70 lbs.

[12]Kas.Mss. 40:10:26:1,2; 40:10:29:1; 41:5:16:1; 43:1:28:1.

her own hands and not only hired Jean Chapron to go to the post of the Ouias, but went there herself in the pirogue to trade.[13]

A few of the Illinois Indians hired out as voyageurs. Penchirois, said to be from the Xavier mission located on the Michigamia reserve,[14] signed on as a voyageur with Jacque Boutin to go to Detroit and back. The son of an early convert, Jean Saguingora, appears in several contracts. In 1739 he agreed to work for Pierre Chabot, a voyageur/merchant, on a trip from Kaskaskia to the coast. He was to receive a wage of 205 livres, tobacco during the trip, and the cost of his washing in New Orleans. He was hired by other traders as well, and in 1744 made a partnership agreement with Jean Marie Nolan (who was described as a voyageur upriver from Montreal) and Jacque Duchoquet of Kaskaskia for hunting on the upper Mississippi river.[15]

The records show that paddling was only part of a voyageur's work. Men often were hired specifically for hunting; venison from the deer was preserved and the hides tanned. Furs, hides, and meat also were obtained through trade with the Indians. Deer were the major animals hunted on the east side of the Mississippi River; hunting areas along the streams tributary to the Wabash were specified in some documents. Other hunting grounds were on the west bank of the Mississippi and there, in addition to deer, they obtained buffalo, bear, and wild cat skins. These were shipped to France or traded within the colony.

Meat was an important internal trade item–dried venison and buffalo meat, particularly buffalo tongues. Bear oil was a valuable commodity; it was used to replace expensive imported olive oil. The amount of oil rendered from a fat bear in one instance was said to be 120 *pots*.[16]

One of the more unusual demands on voyageurs for work was in 1739 when an attack was planned on Chickasaw Indian villages in retaliation for a French defeat. The governor at New Orleans, Bienville, arranged for purchase in Illinois of oxen and horses and for them to be taken to Fort St. Francois, which was located in present Tennessee. Contracts were made with voyageurs to act as herders for these animals. The oxen were under the supervision of Raphael Beauvais, and the horses under Jean Potier. Altogether forty-five Frenchmen and seventeen Indians (including Jean Saguingora) were hired.

The drive was not a success; some of the stock were lost enroute. Even before the drive reached Fort St. Francois, a contract was made with Philippe Chauvin *dit* Joyeuse to recover the strays. His wages were said to be contingent upon the number of animals he found; there is no record of how many he recovered.[17]

---

[13] Kas. Mss. 40:7:26:1; 41:9:22:1; 37:10:9:1.

[14] The Michigamia reserve was located between Fort de Chartres and St. Phillipe.--Ed.

[15] Kas. Mss.43:11:15:1; 39:2:27:1; 44:6:10:1.

[16] Seymour Feiler, ed., *Travels in the Interior of North American 1751-1762* (Norman: University of Oklahoma Press, 1962), 118.

[17] Margaret K. Brown, "Allons Cowboys!," *Journal of the Ill. State Historical Society* 76 (1983) : 4.

transport was by pirogue. Pirogues were large dugout canoes fashioned from the huge trees of the virgin forest, forty to fifty feet long and three to five feet wide. The pirogues had a rudder and often a sail; some could carry thirty men. Larger boats--small flatbottomed boats called bateaux-- were made of planks; bateaux seem to have been built to a standard size of forty by nine feet.[17]

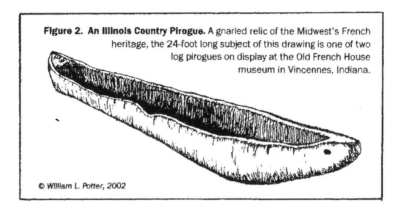

Figure 2. An Illinois Country Pirogue. A gnarled relic of the Midwest's French heritage, the 24-foot long subject of this drawing is one of two log pirogues on display at the Old French House museum in Vincennes, Indiana.

© William L. Potter, 2002

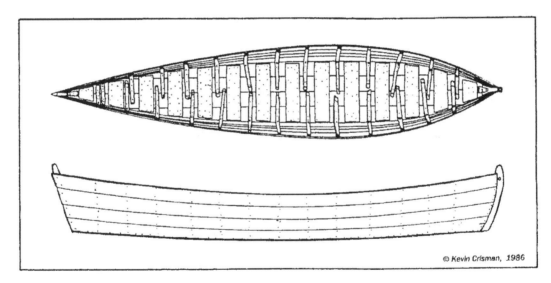

© Kevin Crisman, 1986

Figure 3. An 18th Century Batteau. These plans represent a batteau recovered archeologically from Lake George in New York. It is believed to have been part of a massive fleet built for the British military in 1758, but later scuttled; several of the craft were found.

[Courtesy Dr. Kevin Crisman, Texas A&M.]

---

[17]Gilles Proulx, *Between France and New France: Life Abroad the Tall Sailing Ships* (Louisiana: State University Press, 1963).

Contracts for construction of both pirogues and bateaux are given in the Kaskaskia records. Jean Baptiste LeComte agreed to build a pirogue of black poplar wood forty feet long, three feet wide, and able to carry 7000-8000 livres. The boat was to have a rudder, three oars, and one paddle. A pirogue of cottonwood and three oars were part of a price recorded in a land sale. Another pirogue was to hold 14 to 15,000 livres burden and to be able to carry 12,000 livres of flour;[19] it was to be fully rigged with a cover for the flour. This pirogue was to be delivered to Fort de Chartres all loaded and ready to leave for New Orleans.[20]

The boats also used sails when possible. In the inventory of the last Fort de Chartres two boat sails with their ropes and four other sails are listed. Four awnings for boats are given as well.[21]

Michel Vien and Michel Le Jeune, partners, agreed to build a bateau of walnut of 30,000 livres burden for Louis Jiscart *dit* Benoist. Again the buyer agreed to supply nails, and he also provided two men to assist in the project. A bateau took longer to build, and the workers were given from December to the beginning of April for completion. For wages they would receive 500 livres of grain and five *pots* of brandy.[22]

Another document is not clear about what type of craft is being constructed. Jean Aubuchon, who is listed as a boat builder from Kaskaskia, contracted to build two boats for the partners Andre Roy and Jacque Godefroy, voyageurs/traders of Detroit Erie. The partners were to furnish the nails and other necessary ironwork. The agreement stated that each boat should be capable of carrying 17,000 livres load in addition to men and supplies. The contract for the work was made in November and the boats were to be completed by the end of January. The nails would suggest that it is a bateau. In the document one description of it is *voiture de port*, but then it states that Aubuchon's wage was to be 600 livres for each pirogue.[23]

On a notary's list there is a reference to a document no longer extant that contracted for five bateaux for the king to be made by Baptiste Aubuchon. Baptiste is probably the same person referred to as Jean in the previous documents; Jean Baptiste was a very common name.[24]

The dates of the contracts hiring voyageurs reflect the seasonal activities of the trade. Voyages to New Orleans were made mainly in the spring and fall. Going down in the spring when the river was swift, high, and flooded over its banks helped keep hostile Indians at a distance. In autumn when the river was low and less rapid, paddling was easier upstream, but the danger of Indian attack was greater. The

---

[19] The livre was used both as a measure of weight and a monetary unit. As a weight it is roughly equivalent to a pound. As a monetary unit there were 20 sous to the livre. It is not possible to give equivalences in modern money.

[20] Kas. Mss. 26:8:12:1; 25:5:7:1; 33:9:2:1.

[21] James F. Keefe, "The Inventory of Fort de Chartres," *Muzzleloader*, January./February. 1992

[22] Kas. Mss. 37:12:16:1; the boat is called in this document *voiture de port*.

[23] Kas. Mss. 46:11:22:1.

[24] Kas. Mss. 56:10:8:1.

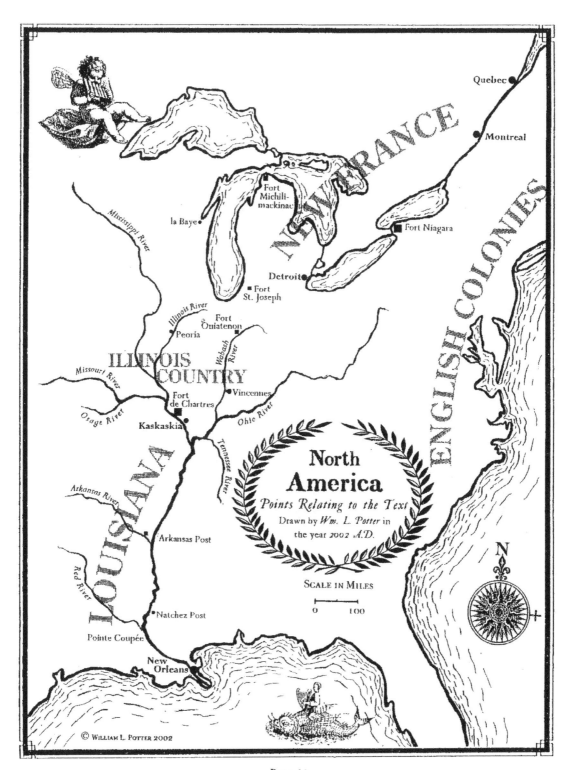

North
America
Points Relating to the Text
Drawn by *Wm. L. Potter* in
the year *2002 A.D.*

SCALE IN MILES

0   100

© WILLIAM L. POTTER 2002

majority of the contracts for trips to New Orleans were made between April and June. Most contracts made in the Illinois were to work the trip from Kaskaskia to New Orleans and back, but voyageurs were hired for one way also.

Trading up the Missouri River was less tied to the seasons, although most contracts were made toward the end of the summer. Workers generally were hired to work for ten to twelve months at the post. The few contracts in the Kaskaskia collection relating to Detroit and Michilimackinac were made in the winter months. Hunting contracts were written towards the end of the summer for the voyageurs to go out in the fall. Meat and hides could be prepared then and the meat salted down for transport to various posts. Bear were captured in winter months as they were fat then and could be rendered for a good supply of oil.

Jacque Boutin agreed in a contract at the end of July in 1739 to go from Kaskaskia to the hunting grounds with La Fleur and then to New Orleans. His duties were mostly to be transporting and salting meat killed by La Fleur.[25]

By November of 1743 he was hiring helpers and Jean Baptiste Sans Soucy agreed to go with him to Detroit. As wages Sans Soucy was to receive leggings and half of the pelts that he (San Soucy) hunted.[26] Michel Le Cour hired Louis Vallee in September for a trip from Missouri to Michilimackinac for a wage of 300 livres in beaver or other pelts, leggings, and two buckskins for moccassins. He was also allowed to bring back a small amount of merchandise.[27]

Official convoys of boats were sent downriver to New Orleans at least twice a year by the commandant at Fort de Chartres. The Fort's commandant issued an official announcement about the projected departure of a convoy:

> *Notice to everyone who wishes to do down to the sea and to send their goods in the boats of the King, to appear by Monday the sixth of May at Fort de Chartres to give an account of the goods which will be sent in the said boats to Mr. de La Bussoniere and De La Loere Flaucour.*[28]

Flour, lead, hides, and other commodities went down on the official convoys, and manufactured items imported from France were brought back up. The materials obtained in New Orleans were placed in the King's storehouse at the Fort. These items were distributed in various ways; gifts were given to the Indians from the government allotment, and the storehouse was a resource for the local inhabitants. The farmers brought in flour, grain, and other products to exchange for the goods. Unfortunately, the role of the fort in the trade network is obscured because of the lack of governmental records.

Besides the items that they already had traded at the Fort for goods, the local people could send their own produce downriver to trade in New Orleans, so along

---

[25] Kas. Mss. 39:7:31:1.
[26] Kas. Mss. 43:11:17:1.
[27] Kas. Mss. 37:9:23:2.
[28] Kas. Mss. 37:5:4:2, trans by Lawrie Dean.

with the convoy went the pirogues owned by individuals. A convoy might have twenty to thirty boats, both government and privately owned. An individual taking advantage of the safety of a convoy was Joseph Desruissiaux, who hired Jean Baptiste Amiot to go with him in the convoy for the salary of 100 livres and one month's lodging in New Orleans. Amiot's employment was to begin fifteen days before the departure of the convoy; part of his duties must have been to prepare and load the boat.[29]

Individuals with their pirogues found the easiest and safest trips were to go down with the official convoy in the spring and back with the autumn one. This sequence is reflected in voyageur agreements. In one contract a man was hired to go to New Orleans; he would *"return from the sea in the autumn of this year"*. Another man was to come *"back with the spring convoy"*. Not all waited in New Orleans for that length of time, though, so boats did go up and down throughout the year depending on the weather. Sometimes convoys went up in late summer, but this was said not to be the best time- *"There is a difficulty in sending a convoy in the summer because the heat makes the crews fall sick and that causes considerable delays..."*[30]

The trip downstream took between twelve and twenty-five days and required the efforts of about twenty-five to thirty men. The return trip against the current took three to four months. An upriver government convoy in 1737 required eighty men to row the various boats--twenty-four French soldiers, ten Swiss, and the rest were hired voyageurs and blacks. In 1748 (when war was on) the convoy was said to need 150 to 200 men; the majority were for protection.[31]

The convoys were lead by a commander who was appointed in New Orleans. There were frequent complaints about these men and their behavior. Often they used goods for their own purposes and dawdled along, more interested in convivial evening than in progress upriver.

> *Having arrived at the Natchez, Monsieur de Tonty had some brandy drawn from two casks, ...afterwards de Tonty forced the Sieur Dessessards and Paschal to fill the said casks with water from the Mississippi.*

> *But the true reason is ... the small authority which the officers have over the soldiers and inhabitants, and the familiarity with which some officers too indiscreetly drink with them. M. de Montchervaux is among these. It is a rare occurrence when rum does not deprive him of reason at least once a day in such company.*[32]

---

[29]Kas. Mss. 48:5:19:1.

[30]Dunbar Rowland and A.G. Sanders, eds., *Mississippi Provincal Archives: French Dominion, 1704-1743* [Hereafter cited as MPA]; 3 vols. (Jackson, Mississippi:, , 1917-32), 3:626

[31]N.M. Miller Surrey, *The Commerce of Louisiana during the French Regime, 1699-1763.* Studies in History, Economics and Public Law, Vol.71:1, whole #167 (New York: Columbia University, 1916), 74-75.

[32]Margaret K. Brown and Lawrie Cena Dean, *The Village of Chartres in Colonial Illinois, 1720-1765*

The officials in New Orleans tended to excuse the persons and suggestions in the early 1750s to have the convoys privatized and put up for auction did not come about. Despite any problems, there was more safety for the pirogues with the convoy.

A more efficient trip upriver--but with other problems--was described by Diron D'Artaguiette in his journal in the mid-1720s. D'Artaguiette departed from New Orleans on December twenty-second in a boat manned by nine soldiers and five sailors; it was equipped with a sail. They were accompanied by Indians and a pirogue belonging to Dulongpré from Illinois carrying six voyageurs. On January sixth, having reached the Red River, they were joined by a pirogue rowed by seven men with Fr. Boulanger of the Illinois Jesuit mission returning to Kaskaskia with supplies.

> *Jan. 9 - The salt meat which we brought for ourselves and our crew has given out. Our hunter does not kill anything and we have no hope of getting food until we reach the Yazous.*
> *Jan. 23- a good wind from the south assisted us until evening...*
> *Jan. 24- The stiff breeze holding, we came by dinner time without rowing to the Petit Gouffre, which is a bluff where a great eddy is formed, which is very dangerous when the waters are high...*
> *Jan. 29- Strong currents, together with a violent north wind...*
> *Feb. 8- All the past night it did not stop raining, and, the rain continuing, we have been obliged to stay here...*
> *Feb. 9- The rain fell all the past night and continued this morning, which obliged us to remain here.*
> *Feb. 10- The rain having ceased, we continued our journey, and, 3 leagues[33] above, we found seven pirogues loaded with meat which Canadian traders, established at the Ilinnois, are taking down to New Orleans to sell.*
> *Feb. 11- Weather fair and cold. We remained here with the canoes of the Canadians to dry our clothes which were wet through and through.*

On February 14th a voyageur, Legras (from the pirogue of Dulongpré) and an Indian left to hunt and did not return. The convoy camped and they fired guns to signal them. When they had not returned by the 16t,h Dulongpré sent four of his men in the pirogue to search for them, but to no avail. The level of the river rose eight feet in the night.

> *Feb. 17- We are in great need of meat. Our men begin to grumble and our Indian has hunted without having killed anything, which has determined us to leave for*

(New Orleans: Polyanthos Press, 1977), K444. Theodore Pease and Ernestine Jenison, eds., *Illinois on the Eve of the Seven Years War*, in Illinois State Historical Library, *Collections of the Illinois State Historical Library*, (Springfield: Illinois State Historical Library, 1940), 29:157, 273.

[33]A league frequently is given as 2.5 miles, but it was a highly variable measure in those days. On the trip the maximum distance travelled in one day was eight leagues, but the average was three to four leagues.

Grand Pointe Coupée to endeavor to kill some buffaloes, for we are reduced to Indian corn, without either meat or flour...

By February 18th the missing men had not appeared; D'Artaguiette sent out nine Frenchmen and four Indians in the Jesuit's pirogue. This time they were successful and found the two men floating on a raft they had made.

Feb. 20- The past night the water rose four feet.
Feb. 21- At daybreak the Rev. Jesuit Father said mass, after which we embarked and continued our journey, killed two ducks...Today the water rose four feet.

On February 22nd they went up the Arkansas River a few miles, camped, and killed two more ducks. The river rose seven feet. A few days later one of the men in the Jesuit's canoe deserted and disappeared into the wilderness.

March 3- We departed early in the morning in company with the Reverend Jesuit Father and Dulongpré, to each of whom we had to give a man as otherwise they would not have been able to follow us.

On the third and fifth of March D'Artaguiette noted that each night the river had risen six feet; however, on the seventh it began to drop and receded half a foot; from then on it dropped slowly but steadily. The Indians all left the convoy at the Arkansas.

March 18- A violent north wind blew the past night which increased this morning...This had decided us to remain here.
March 19- Weather gloomy and cold...about noon it began to snow.
March 22- The thunder, lightning and rain continued all of the past night. At 10 o'clock in the morning the rain ceased. The weather was still cloudy and cold. We were obliged to remain, the winds having gone around to the north and becoming violent.
March 28- We remained here to celebrate the holy Easter festival and to give time to our men to make their devotions. The Reverend Father said high mass for us this morning, and, after noon, vespers. There were only two men in our boat who did not take communion.
March 31-...we met seven pirogues full of traders living among the Ilinnois, who had been hunting in the Riviere de Ouabache. They are loaded with salt meat and bear oil, which they are going to sell at New Orleans. They were not able to tell us any news from the Ilinnois as it had been four months since they left there.
April 9- Weather clear and cold. We have been obliged to remain here so as to make oars and to give our men some rest.

This trip was not endangered by any Indian attacks, but ambushes were one of the greatest hazards of a voyage. At several points along the way the crew related to D'Artaguiette events that previously had happened at that locale. At Ecores a

Prud'homme the Langevins, father and son, had been captured by the Chickasaws. Later the crew ate dinner at the place where Chesne and an Arkansas Indian had been killed. About four leagues above the Ouabache was where the Sioux had killed Desnepeu, his wife, and two children.

They reached the Ohio River (Ouabache)[34] April 12th. After this there were no heavy currents as it was the Ouabache that was high and the Mississippi was very low. On April 17th they finally arrived at Kaskaskia.[35]

Capture by Indians or death from their attacks was common. Convoys generally were too large and well manned, but small groups of pirogues were severely in danger; even going with a convoy was not always a guarantee of safety. In 1741 a convoy of three bateaux (with twenty-eight men in each) and a number of pirogues headed upstream at the end of August. Antoine Bonnefoy, an *engagé*,[36] wrote in his journal about events. The pirogue in which Bonnefoy paddled was commanded by Legras; that pirogue and another belonging to Marin followed the convoy until the bateaux crossed to the western side of the Mississippi near the Ouabache River. Although the commander of the bateaux signaled for them to come along too, they decided to stay on the opposite bank. They saw a number of pirogues by the bank and thought that they belonged to Illinois or Missouri Indians. However, this proved to be incorrect; they were Cherokees'. The two pirogues (with eight men each) were ambushed. In the first boat the helmsman Legras and two men were killed; two men in Marin's boat were injured but they were further out on the river and were able to escape. The Indians surrounded the first pirogue and seized the remaining four Frenchmen and a black man. The other men were Joseph Rivard, Pierre Coussot, and "*Guillaume Potier, half-breed, son of Potier, habitant of the Illinois, and Legra's negro.*" The black's name was not given. Although the bateaux were in sight of the battle, the commander took no action to help them, probably fearing that a larger force of Indians was nearby.

The Indians did not harm them, they merely tied the hands of the Frenchmen and took them up the Ouabache, then down the Tennessee River. The Frenchmen were kept in a village and adopted by Indians there. The black man had been injured in the original fight and finally died. In the village they found other captured Frenchmen, a son of André Crespe, and Jean Arlois, *engagés* of Turpin who had been there for a year. The Cherokees in that attack had killed twenty-five out of the twenty-eight voyageurs in the pirogues. The voyageurs had tried to urge the Indians to make peace with the French, but the three British traders resident in the village instigated the Indians to continue warfare.

---

[34] The lower Ohio River--the portion between the Wabash and the Mississippi rivers--was thought of by some Illinois French residents (and even a few mapmakers) as part of the Wabash ("Ouabache") River, with the Ohio its tributary, rather than the other way around. An example of this can be seen on the 1733 Renaut map, *Partie Des Illinnois*, appearing in: Wayne C. Temple, ed., *Indian Villages of the Illinois Country Atlas Supplement* (Springfield: Illinois State Museum, 1975), map 68. The "Ouabache" mentioned in this instance clearly refers to the lower Ohio River--Ed.

[35] Newton D. Mereness, ed., *Travels in the American Colonies* (New York: MacMillan Co., 1916).

[36] A person who made an *engagement*, a contractual agreement, in this case to serve as a voyageur.

In April, when the Indians were having a drunken celebration, all the Frenchmen escaped, except for Guillaume Potier who was drinking with the Indians. They made a raft, but it soon struck a sunken tree; Arlois and Coussot caught hold of the tree; Bonnefoy was carried on by the current for quite a distance. When he reached shore he fired shots to let them know where he was, but they did not appear. Bonnefoy ended up at an Alabama Indian village and finally back at a French post. The fate of the others is unknown.[37]

Complications of all sorts could attend the trading voyages. One such problem can be partly reconstructed from depositions taken for legal action; the documentation is incomplete so the circumstances are not altogether clear. Other similar complaints appear scattered through the manuscripts; what follows is the most complete example of a such case.

Antoine Bienvenu of Kaskaskia had gone down to New Orleans to trade and was preparing to return to the Illinois when he became ill. Another trader, Mathurin, took Jean Rocher, who was the employee of a third trader, La Bossiere, and started back upriver with Bienvenu's goods. Bienvenu was to catch up with them at Pointe Coupée. When Mathurin reached the small settlement of De Noyon, he unloaded a barrel of Bienvenu's wine because the pirogue was overloaded. At Pointe Coupée La Bossiere and Rocher purchased another pirogue to relieve the overloading, and La Bossiere hired his own men. Bienvenu joined the group at Pointe Coupée in his pirogue, and he and Mathurin left together. One of La Bossiere's men fell ill and he asked Bienvenu and Mathurin to lend him one. Exchange of personnel seems to be characteristic of the voyages; whoever was in need was supported.

Shortly after leaving Pointe Coupée the pirogues were attacked by hostile Indians. The details are not clear from the depositions, but Mathurin was captured and apparently killed. Another voyageur, Francois Baron *dit* La Liberte (who had been hired jointly by Mathurin and Bienvenu), was badly injured. Bienvenu had, or felt he had, an obligation to pay for Baron's medical expenses and to take care of him for the rest of his life. Later Baron recovered and discharged Bienvenu from this obligation.

The legal disputes centered around various goods that had been lost, disposed of, or possibly taken by the attacking Indians. Bienvenu stated that he had sent back to Pointe Coupée in a pirogue four *pots* and two barrels of brandy and one butt of wine belonging to Mathurin. The rest of Mathurin's effects were left there also. The remainder of the property in the pirogue was said to belong to La Bossiere; some articles were taken by De La Houssaye as payment at Pointe Coupée. The pirogue or pirogues that returned to Pointe Coupée after the attack later must have been paddled up to the Illinois, for La Bossiere's property arrived at Kaskaskia.

In April of 1740 La Bossiere filed a claim against Bienvenu in the Superior Court in New Orleans. He stated he had arranged with Bienvenu and Mathurin for passage by dugout canoe to Illinois, but due to various mishaps and by Bienvenu's fault he lost 3845 livres and demanded 300 livres in damages as well.

---

[37]Mereness 1961.

Perhaps the Indians did not get any of the materials; otherwise it is difficult to see why Bienvenu would be at fault. However, the decision in the case is not known.[38]

The dangers that could be expected on the voyages caused many men to make wills before leaving. Antoine Ossant, a trader about to start out on a long journey, made a will giving everything to Joseph Braseau and his wife.[39] Francois Valle of Kaskaskia, who was planning to go to the Wabash, made his will leaving 1000 livres to the church of the Immaculate Conception in Kaskaskia, 1000 livres to Jean Baptiste Gouin *dit* Champagne, master smith of Fort de Chartres, 500 livres to Francois Corset *dit* Coco of Kaskaskia, 1000 livres to Pierre Chauret, his cousin, 1500 livres to any of his brothers who might come to the Illinois, and the remainder to his partner, Joseph Liberville *dit* Joson.[40] Louis Longuin made a will in anticipation of his trip upriver to the Fox Indians with Marin Urtebise. Longuin returned from the trip but brought back for inventory the goods of his employer Urtebise, who had died there.[41]

Another hazard of the trip that all complained about and no one could do much about were the mosquitoes. Breeding prolifically in the marshes and bayous of the Mississippi, they swarmed over the voyageurs, who had to make a choice between sweltering with the heat under covers or suffering with their flesh exposed to the hordes. The mosquitoes were so numerous that the Indians who went to Paris in 1725, could only try to convey the vast number of people in the city by saying there were as many as "*mosquitoes in the woods*."[42]

The voyageur's wages offered for the trip to New Orleans and back during the period 1737 to 1743 averaged between 200 and 225 livres; from 1743 to 1748, 300 to 325 livres. The difference may be due to inflation, or to a shift to largely "cash" pay. Many contracts in the earlier period specified in addition to cash a number of other items as part of the wage, whereas in the later times it was a wage and the right to carry goods in the boat that predominated.

Items requested as part of the wage varied. One man wanted a cask of brandy, cloth for a capot, four shirts, a hat, a pair of stockings, and a pair of shoes. A number of men wanted to be supplied with as many moccasins as they would need during the trip. Others requested buckskins for shoes, probably again referring to moccasins as the heavier cattle hides would have been used for other shoes. Leggings were part of the contract for some. One man specified that his employer would arrange to have his washing done for him in New Orleans.[43]

The amount of wages depended in part upon the extent of the work designated in the contract. If the man was going to hunt with his employer, salt the meat, and

---

[38]Kas. Mss. 39:9:23:2 and others cited there.

[39]Kas. Mss. 46:4:27:1.

[40]Kas. Mss. 46:4:27:2.

[41]Kas. Mss. 47:10:17:1.

[42]Reuben Gold Thwaites, ed., *Jesuit Relations and Allied Documents*, 73 vols. (Cleveland: Burrows Bros. Co., 1896-1901), 68: 213.

[43]Kas. Mss. 31:-:-:1; 37:9:23:2; 46:7:9:1; 39:8:11:1; 43:11:17:1; 39:2:27:1. Moccasins were called "souliers sauvage".

then transport it to the coast for sale, he received a higher wage than if he was just transporting hides downriver. Travel to the nearby Wabash paid less than the trip to New Orleans, although distance might not have been the only factor. Wages for Detroit were about the same as to New Orleans.

The long trip to Michilimackinac also may have paid less, but at least one of the existing contracts was a hire for one way only. Antoine Maniere *dit* La Bastille agreed to go with Pierre Dutailly to Michilimackinac for a wage of 150 livres. His service was to end when the merchandise was unloaded and stored in Dutailly's house at Michilimackinac.[44] The sample of contracts available for places other than New Orleans is too small for any definitive statement on cost.

Table 1 gives a list of the places that voyageurs contracted to go. More than one destination might be specified in the contract, for example, to go to the hunting grounds and then to New Orleans, so the total is greater than the number of contracts located.

Table 1

Destinations in Contracts

Canada	2	Michilimackinac	4
Detroit	3	Missouri	8
Fox	3	New Orleans	31
Hunting	13	Ouias	4
Other	10		

Defining actual monetary values is difficult. The causes for the variations in pay for what sounds like the same work cannot be ascertained now. Several possible reasons can be put forth--some men probably were acknowledged to be better workers than others, some might be keener bargainers, or have specially needed skills, or there might have been a temporary shortage of labor.

The term cash in the contract generally did not mean coin. Coinage was scarce in Louisiana; much of it went back to France to pay debts there. The colony's monetary system was very unstable; the Louisiana government was forced to issue various kinds of paper money, including card money-- playing cards with notations of denomination. The paper money fluctuated in value, and counterfeiting was prevalent. In an effort to control this, paper money was recalled frequently and replaced with a new issue. Spanish coins obtained through Florida or other contacts also were used as currency. The relative value of *piastres* versus the French money is shown in a few documents. A debt of 666 livres, 10 sols to Joseph Liberville *dit* Joson,

---

[44]Kas. Mss. 41:2:18:1.

trader of Kaskaskia was to be paid in *piastres* at 100 sols to the *piastre*. Boutin received a letter of exchange from Charles Braseaux for 3000 livres or 600 *piastres*.[45]

The value of items varied with location; distance producing a higher mark-up. Contracts sometimes specified what locational value was to be placed on the wage: "*to be paid in New Orleans in money or dry goods at port prices;*" or "*a wage of fifty livres in pelts at Detroit prices*". The possible variation in prices is shown in one document, "*Thiberge will deliver 1200 livres in merchandise at New Orleans prices to Kaskaskia for 1600 livres in cash,*" although this difference might be also cartage.[46]

In addition to furs, hides, and meat, other materials were shipped downriver. Lead mined in Missouri was exported to France and also traded internally with the posts along the river and in New Orleans. The lead was formed into sheets for transport. The maximum production of the mines was 40,000 livres annually; in 1743, 30,000 livres were shipped to France as ballast.[47]

As farming developed in the rich bottomlands, food products became an important internal trade item, especially flour. Thousands of pounds of flour were transported downriver to the other settlements annually. Wheat--winter wheat in the earlier years and then mainly spring-planted wheat--was ground to flour in watermills, horsemills and windmills. Flour also was processed in a bolting mill; this separated the bran and produced white flour.

Contracts made for delivering flour indicate the quantities desired at the various posts. La Croix agreed to furnish 8715 livres of flour and 215 livres of bacon to New Orleans; enroute he was to leave at the Natchez post 2715 livres of flour and 215 livres of bacon, and at Arkansas post 6000 livres of flour. This quantity could have been transported in a couple of bateaux or three pirogues.

Individual pirogue loads are suggested by other contracts; Thomas Chauvin was to transport 5905 livres of flour to Natchez. Jacques de la Boucherie was to bring to New Orleans 8148 livres of salted beef and thirty-five tongues; Jean Chauvin was to supply 3088 livres of buffalo meat and sixty salted tongues.[48]

The pelts that were traded came from a variety of animals; quantities are given in a few documents. Marin Urtebise received and owed Jacque Grignon for:

> *30 packets of beaver weighing 80 livres*
> *3 packets of wildcat containing 120 pelts*
> *2 packets of bear each of 20 skins*
> *1 packet of 50 otter skins, back and belly.* [49]

---

[45]Kas. Mss. 46:7:30:1; 46:8:6:1.

[46]Kas. Mss. 38:4:29:2; 46:1:3:2; 41:5:23:1.

[47]Norman W. Caldwell, , *The French in the Mississippi Valley, 1740-1750* (Urbana: University of Illinois Press, 1941), 47.

[48]*Louisiana Historical Quarterly.* [Cited hereafter as LHQ], (Various vols. and #s, 1917-1927), 8:290, 3:378, 381.

[49]Kas. Mss. 47:7:12:1.

Jean Dubois owed a debt to Jean Baptiste Alarie for:

> *848 livres of tanned buckskins at 20 sols a livre*
> *120 wildcat at 10 sols the livre*
> *120 livres of dry beaver at 30 sols the livre.*[50]

Nicolas Janisse, voyageur of Kaskaskia, agreed to take charge of pelts belonging to Louis Bienvenu *dit* Delisle during his absence in Detroit. For a wage of 350 livres Janisse said he would protect the pelts from mites, insects, and other dangerous vermin. An inventory of the pelts was made:

> *1156 cats large and small*
> *1160 bear large and small*
> *36 others*
> *134 fox*
> *5 wolves*
> *446 livres of beaver in five packets*
> *448 livres of deerskins in five packets*
> *5 green skins*[51]

These were items taken down to New Orleans; in the return shipping brandy was an important item. Voyageur contracts often contained permission from the employer to bring back brandy in the boat. Much of this brandy probably was destined for the Indian trade despite the frequent rulings against selling liquor to the Indians. Brandy was traded with other Frenchmen, too, and some used for personal consumption.

The quantity shipped most often was expressed in terms of *pots*. The amount requested for transport varied from one to seventy *pots*. Brandy was shipped in various sized containers. A document mentions a barrel[52] of twenty *pots* (about ten gallons); another, three casks,[53] each containing sixty-six to sixty-eight *pots* (thirty-three to thirty-four gallons). The cost is totally confusing due to the intricacies of the debt and wage structures.

In one case 1100 livres was to be repaid by two barrels. An additional ten *pots* were added to the debt and to redeem the debt now 1500 livres, 250 *pots* were required. This makes 10 *pots* equal to 400 livres. In one account 100 *pots* was an indebtedness for 300 livres of buckskin and 125 livres cash, but in another record 100 *pots* was equal to 1348 livres 10 sols in a letter of exchange. At an auction of a

---

[50]Kas. Mss. 47:4:18:1.
[51]Kas. Mss.45:4:28:1.
[52]Kas. Mss. 31:6:24:1, *barique*.
[53]Kas. Mss. 48:3:22:1, *tierson*.

voyageur's goods one man paid 2310 livres for a *pot* of brandy; it must have been a very fine year--or an error in transcription by the notary.[54]

Certain traders and voyageurs were described as "upriver"; this meant that they went north of Kaskaskia to Detroit, Michilimackinac or Montreal. For example, Jean Baptiste Richard, called a voyageur and merchant upriver, contracted with Etienne Couvent to go with him as a voyageur to the Ouias and Miami, and then to return to Kaskaskia. Another voyageur, Louis Bossiere, was hired by Richard for a round trip to Canada. Louis Bienvenu Delisle, described as a trader/voyageur upriver, hired Louis Bohemier as a voyageur to accompany him to Detroit and return.[55]

Since the official records from Fort de Chartres are missing, there is little information about the trade centers controlled through the fort. From the personal documents in existence it appears that leases for trading posts with the Ouia, Miami, Osage, and other nearby Indians were ones given out by the commandant at Fort de Chartres. The only information about their cost is from a memoir of Bougainville that said in reference to the Fort:

> *This post is exploited by licenses whose price is 600 francs per canoe, the voyageur having 300 francs wt. for the ordinary gratifications.*[56]

For a time Jean Baptiste Mallet had the lease of the Miami post. Joseph Bissonet, a voyageur upriver, was to accompany Mallet to New Orleans for supplies and trade goods, then to go to the Miami, winter in Kaskaskia with him, and finally return to New Orleans with the furs and hides.[57]

The post on the Missouri river traded with the Osages; it was licensed to various individuals over the years: Jean Baptiste Poudret, Louis Chapeau, Charles Reaume, Jean Chapron and company, Joseph Desruisseaux, and Joseph Le Duc.

Many of the documents about trade in the Kaskaskia Manuscripts concern debt. The notes of debt--the IOUs--could be transferred from one individual to another; they were a medium of payment and exchange. These notes also were listed in the estate inventories as money due the deceased or as his debts.

Transfers of these IOUs could become quite complicated. In May of 1740 Pierre Messager promised to deliver to Pierre Bouvier upon his return from New Orleans 180 *pots* of brandy and the material to make a complete suit of camelot[58] of silk, including a green coat and two pairs of breeches, one fine half beaver hat, four fine shirts trimmed with good cambric, and a pair of silk hose of a color suitable to the rest.

Messager apparently brought back only part of the agreed upon materials. By March of 1741 Bouvier had received ninety-three and a half *pots* and two shirts.

[54]Kas. Mss. 41:1:10:l; 42:6:15:1; 41:4:20:4; 41:6:9:2; Brown and Dean 1977, K355.

[55]Kas. Mss.39:2:23:1; 37:3:23:1; 47:4:19:1.

[56]Thwaites 1908, 176.

[57]Kas. Mss. 40:4:30:2.

[58]Camelot or camleteen is woolen cloth woven with mohair or silk.

Bouvier then transferred Messager's obligation for the remainder of the brandy and the suit to Antoine Maignon. As no suit had been supplied, arbiters were appointed to discuss the debt, and they gave the decision that Messager owned Bouvier 300 livres for the undelivered suit; this amount was now to be paid to Maignon. However, before any payment was made, the note was transferred again; in May, Maignon gave it to Rene Roy. Then Messager agreed that he would pay Roy 400 livres, or in the event of Messager's death before this payment, a yoke of oxen would be given to him. As complicated as this sounds, Messager had other financial arrangements with property that were even more complex.[59]

A less involved transfer (and a more common type) was that of Pierre Miette, voyageur in the Illinois, who transferred a note of debt he had received from Jean Baptiste Texier of 791 livres 10 sols to Charles Joudouin, voyageur of Kaskaskia, who paid that amount in full to Miette.[60]

Another was:

> *Order by Joseph Buchet, Royal Attorney, that Louis Trudeau pay 1505 livres to Jacques Godefroy of Kaskaskia, in payment of a note made by Jacques Boutin in that amount to Godefroy on Feb. 7, 1746. Because Boutin is now permanently in New Orleans and because Trudeau is obligated to Boutin for 2060 livres, Trudeau is ordered to pay Godefroy, thus reducing his debt to Boutin by the amount paid to Godefroy.*[61]

Boutin illustrates the peripatetic lifestyle of the traders. Boutin was an upriver trader. In 1743 he was said to be residing in Prairie La Magdalene in Canada and trading to Detroit, Michilimackinac, and the Ouias. He had a *congé* for trade out of Kaskaskia, and he hired voyageurs there. By 1746 he was living in Detroit and trading downstream from Kaskaskia to New Orleans. A year later he apparently transferred his operations to New Orleans.[62]

Another upriver trader licensed from Canada was Marin Urtebise of Montreal. Between 1737 and 1750, records reveal his activities, sometimes as an individual trader and at other times in partnership with another person. In 1746 he acknowledged a debt to Jacque Grignon for trade goods he had received, since he was about to go and trade with the Fox Indians. He continued to trade with the Fox until he was killed in 1750; it is not known if they were responsible for his death.

Urtebise not only took trade goods to the Fox, but he provided them with the services of a smith. A smith was very important for the Indians as he could repair their guns, traps, and other iron implements. Jean Baptiste Amoith (called a master smith) from Fort de Chartres agreed to go with Urtebise for a year. Urtebise was to provide him with iron, steel, and a helper. The following year the helper turned out

---

[59] Kas. Mss. 40:5:10:1; 41:3:7:1; 41:5:28:2; 41:5:30:1.

[60] Kas. Mss. 43:9:19:2.

[61] Kas. Mss. 47:3:4:1.

[62] Kas. Mss. 43:8:9:1; 46:1:3:2; 47:3:4:1.

to be Michel Durivage, a voyageur, who agreed to go to the Fox for a year. His tools would be supplied for him.

Another voyageur was hired to go along, too--Pierre Le Duc, who had different talents. During the winter, Le Duc was to build a house at the post and a pirogue. At the end of March he was to receive 400 livres and a canoe in which he could return to Kaskaskia alone. At least two other voyageurs were contracted to go along and help, Jean Boudrais and Louis Longuin, to winter there at the Fox post, and collect furs and pelts.[63]

The traders formed an interconnected network. The same names turn up repeatedly in different associations, and it is obvious that, despite being in competition at times, there was also cooperation.

Joseph Desruisseaux was another trader for whom there exists records between 1736 and 1751; he was still alive in 1751, but the Kaskaskia records cease to provide information on his trade beyond that point. In the 1730s he hired voyageurs, even having one, Martial Dufour, agree to donate *"his person, body, goods, labor and industry for his lifetime"* in exchange for food, lodging, and maintenance until his death. The cancellation of this donation is not in the records, but it must have occurred since in 1740 Dufour asked for--and received--a grant of land for a garden, and in 1744 (when he was dying of an illness) named an administrator for his wife.

In the 1730s Desruisseaux was associated with Marin Urtebise in upriver trade, but in the 1740s his main interests seem to have been in another geographical region, the Missouri. His involvement there may have begun earlier; in 1738 there was the resolution of a dispute between he and Poudret, who was at that time the lessee of the Missouri post. Desruisseaux continued his contacts with Urtebise. In 1743 Urtebise testified before the commandant and judge, acquitting Desruisseaux of fault in some case for which the details are not preserved.

By at least 1745, probably even a year earlier, Desruisseaux was the lessee at the post of the Missouri and hired Jean Baptiste Allarie and Guillaume La Douceur to operate the post for him. He agreed to supply them with goods for the post and for trade on the river of the Grand Osages. A military commandant for the Missouri post was sent out from Fort de Chartres with regulations to be followed. These rules limited the trade of the post to the Indians living on the Grand Osage River. The lessees were not to attempt to attract other tribes to come to them, although they could supply other Indians who came to the post, and also provide goods to the voyageurs who dealt with the Little Osages. They were forbidden to buy either Shawnee or Nakitoche slaves.

The post must have been quite profitable. The profits were to be shared half-and-half between Desruisseaux and his agents. The trade goods were to be purchased only from Desruisseaux; however, he was going to provide half of the goods free and pay half of the wages for a helper. He must have expected a considerable mark up and

---

[63]Kas. Mss.46:7:12:1,2; 47:9:10:1; 47:10:14:1,:16:1;:17:1.

return on his investment. What the profit margin was is not known. An earlier document from Montreal reported a profit of 60%.

This helper may have been Amiot, who was hired at that time. This contract is not extant; only a notation on the notary's list exists, so it cannot be determined if Amoit(h) went out to do smithing as he did the following year for Urtebise or not. Perhaps the post was not as lucrative as hoped, or perhaps it was so good that another trader became interested; whatever the reason was, by 1747 Desruisseaux was in partnership with Joseph Le Duc.

In 1746 Joseph Belcour was at the post helping as a trader. In 1747 the agreement with Alarie and La Douceur was cancelled, and Belcour was hired for another year by Le Duc and Company. Belcour was to receive 600 livres of tanned buckskins and six tanned buffalo robes (showing some of the expected returns from the Indians), a pair of leggings, and a tobacco supply. At the end of his term of service DesRusseaux verified that Belcour had received his wages.

About this time Desruisseaux and Le Duc had a disagreement, and the judge, Buchet, appointed Urtebise and Louis Bore to arbitrate the dispute. The partnership was dissolved, and Desruisseaux had to pay Le Duc 1500 livres. Part of Desruisseaux' payment of his debt was in notes owed him by Urtebise and Routtier.

Desruisseaux continued to hold the lease for the Missouri post, and in 1748 rehired Jean Baptiste Amiot as a voyageur and personal helper for a year at the post for 300 livres. In 1750 Desruisseaux and Le Duc renewed their partnership; apparently their differences were forgotten.[64]

Trading as a business involved acquiring goods suitable and desirable for exchange with the Indians. These articles were imported from France and sometimes (when that source was not adequate) from British suppliers. Scattered official complaints from Canada and Louisiana indicated that trade with the British was much more prevalent than would be expected. The voyageurs were interested in a good return on their furs and hides. They were not too fussy about who supplied them; politics was not as important as business. Then, too, sometimes the British goods were of a better quality, and the Indians were quite capable of recognizing this.

The trader/merchant was a businessman. He purchased hides or hired persons to get meat and hides, and contracted with men to assist in carrying these to exchange for new trade supplies. Individual voyageurs could--and did--obtain trade materials. This is how the trader/merchants themselves got their start. The traders were at various levels of prosperity, of course. Some had one or two pirogues; others had bateaux and did a larger volume of business. Some formed partnerships to increase the pool of available cash/credit, but all accompanied their goods to oversee their sale, and probably paddled as well.

The variation in prosperity of voyageurs and traders can be seen in the official inventories that were made of the property they owned when they married, or when a partnership was dissolved, or at their death. An inventory was taken in the early days

---

[64]Kas. Mss. 30:8:12:1; 37:6:19:2; 40:6:28:2; 44:12:16:1; 38:8:23:1; 43:5:31:1; 45:6:28:2; 45:-:-:4; 47:7:1:1; 47:7:4:1; 47:7:10:1; 48:5:19:1; 50:1:14:1.

of the colony for the voyageur/hunter Legras; he was killed by the Cherokee on the trip related by Bonnefoy. This inventory indicates the sparse personal belongings he had left behind at Fort de Chartres:

> *One pot of brandy - three trade guns, one broken - an old blanket of dog hair - an old greatcoat of limbourg - an old pair of silk hose and one of wool - a steel seal - two shirts of linen and three old shirts - a case with two razors - a small syringe - a comb - a pocket knife - two gun worms - half a bar of soap - an old casket without a key and two pairs of Indian moccasins.*[65]

His appearance in the village must have been important to him with his soap, razors, and comb. The above list is from the sale of his goods; presumably his breeches were in too poor shape to be sold or his only pair was with him; none are listed. He probably took very little with him; Canadian authors point out that in the canoes *"the equipment of every voyageur was kept to the minimum, to leave the greatest possible amount of space for the merchandise."*[66]

Michel Le Cour, a trader, became ill and died at Fort de Chartres. An inventory of his goods was taken at the home of Francois Xavier Rollet in Cahokia. Stored in a small trunk was a book of his accounts; he was owed 1190 livres from various people. Michel was literate; his signature appears on other documents. Among his possessions were: a decorated case with four razors, sharpening stone, knife, and scissors. He had a dozen trade knives, a dozen gunflints, two livres of powder, a large gun, and two new carbines.[67] He had 2067 livres of deerskins, and also beaver and bear skins for which no total was given. He owned an Indian slave and her six year old son; these were sold by his executor for 500 livres to pay Michel's medical, funeral, and legal expenses.[68]

Andre Chaverneau, described as a trader/voyageur, died at the home of Jean Baptiste Crely. Some items in his inventory were: two pair of breeches, three shirts, a napkin, a cap, two pairs of wool stockings, an aune[69] of black ribbon, a pair of shoes, and a coat of double serge. He also had a framed mirror, and a rosary with a crucifix, two buckles and five buttons of silver. There were three collars of porcelain (beaded collars for the Indians), a bottle case for four bottles, a large lamp, a wooden plate, a brush, a small trunk covered with hide, and three carrots of tobacco (a carrot is a dried twist of tobacco shaped somewhat like a carrot). He had a surprisingly large amount of coinage, 121 livres in gold and silver. Apparently he participated in the agricultural trade as well; he had 1486 livres of wheat.[70]

---

[65] Brown and Dean 1977, K355.

[66] Ramond Douville and Jacques Casanova, *Daily Life in Early Canada* (New York: MacMillan Co., 1968).

[67] The French is *carabines*. This may mean short guns or guns with rifled barrels.

[68] Kas. Mss. 40:6:4:1,2.

[69] An aune is a cloth measure 1.18 meters in length.

[70] Kas. Mss. 47:9:30:1.

Pierre Dumont *dit* La Violette, a voyageur/trader, wanted to marry Agnes Clement, the widow of another trader, St. Yves. Prior to the marriage an inventory was made of the property that he brought to the marriage community. Pierre owned a house; it was a small one of post-in-the-ground construction, but it had a stone chimney and a shingled roof. His lot was not fenced. He had a yoke of oxen (the eighteenth century equivalent of a tractor), a cow, her calf, and a bull. Some of the possessions listed appear to be his household goods, and others, trade stock. The two large cooking pots, a feather bed, a coverlet of white wool, a pair of breeches of black *calmande*, a pair of shoes, a gun, and an old chest with a key were probably his belongings. The thirty-nine aunes of *haut Brin*, twelve dozen tin spoons, two guns, and twelve livres of lead were trade items. He also was owed 1180 livres by Bienvenu, a prosperous trader.[71]

Antoine de Tonty died at Fort de Chartres in 1737. He had been a voyageur/trader for fifteen to twenty years. He owned a house twenty by fifteen feet in size with a straw roof in poor condition. Some of his other belongings were: two cows, two old guns, andirons, a spit, two candlesticks, candle snuffers, two poor pewter salt cellars, a used half-beaver hat trimmed with silver, an old suit and coat of coffee-colored woolen broadcloth, an old suit and coat of gray woolen broadcloth, an old suit, coat and breeches of camleteen, four carrots of tobacco worth 16 livres ten sols, a mattress, a pillow, a chest without a key, a case for ten flasks (five were broken), eight used shirts, a pair of old sheets, used silk hose, a spade, eighteen pewter plates, and two platters. The total value of his estate was 1070 livres and 10 sols.[72]

The bottle cases mentioned in the inventories were quite common. A case was a large wooden box with a lid; the interior was divided top to bottom with thin wood dividers to hold the square, dark green glass bottles that (because of these boxes) were know as case bottles. The bottles were of various sizes, but generally were about ten inches high. The width was greater at the shoulder, and sometimes indentations were made under the shoulder during its manufacture that facilitated removal from the case.

An inventory of the goods of the wife of the prosperous trader, Desrussieux, included: a Spanish crucible, two large earthen pots, ten earthenware bottles, and three pots in different shapes, an earthenware tankard, a coffee mill, two silver candlesticks with snuffer, a dozen sets of silver tableware, a salt cellar of faience, a pair of silver shoe buckles, two mirrors, seven large coffee cups, a Spanish hat with gold trim, six crystal goblets, a bowl with gold, and a faience pot.[73]

These inventories show the variety and quality of goods available to the population in the Illinois in the eighteenth century. Far from being a primitive pioneer settlement, it was as close to civilized life as it was possible to be in the wilderness. Indeed, for many persons--including voyageurs--prosperity was more

---

[71] Some of the terms for cloth cannot be translated as their meaning is not known. Kas. Mss. 47:9:5:2.
[72] Kas. Mss. 37:6:23:1. Camleteen seems to be the same as camelot.
[73] Kas. Mss. 45:11:3:1.

accessible here than it would have been for them as laborers in France. Life was harsh and dangerous in the New World, but the rewards were worth it.

The number of persons involved directly in trading is impossible to determine. Besides the "merchant/traders" there were many individuals who participated occasionally. The only indication of the quantity of voyageurs comes from the census taken in 1732 that states there were "transients who come and go, about fifty men".[74] The 1740s were the most active and prosperous period, and presumably there were even more persons involved then, but no figures exist.

After 1750 trading did not cease, although the Kaskaskia Manuscripts do not preserve records of trade any more. The French and Indian War (Seven Years War) did cause disruption in the trade--warring Indians and problems with supply particularly. As the hostilities intensified, trade with Canada became more difficult, and then virtually ceased after the British conquest there.

The British took over the Illinois country in 1765; much of the activity shifted to the Spanish west bank. French traders moved there, or worked with trading partners there. Trade continued up and down the Mississippi River. This frustrated the British, who saw most of the fur trade still being taken out of their hands, even though they had won the area by treaty.

It was probably during the British rule that most of the Illinois notaries' records (except for those pertaining to land) were lost or destroyed. Because the major notary list for the period is also missing, the extent of the loss cannot be determined.

Active trading continued in Kaskaskia under the Virginians and Americans. Although the Kaskaskia Manuscripts lack later material, there is extensive documentation from various sources, including the firm of Baynton, Wharton and Morgan (in the Clemens Library, Ann Arbor, Michigan) and the Pierre Menard papers (in the Illinois State Historical Library) which await the thorough study they deserve.

The time span covered by the Kaskaskia Manuscripts voyageur records is brief, but still supplies a glimpse of the trades, the individual traders, hunters, and voyageurs in the mid-eighteenth century. Trade was vital in the economy of the Illinois country, and aspects of it were interwoven into the framework of the society. These documents shed some illumination on the role of the trade, and into the lives to those involved.

---

[74]Archives Nationales des Colonies, C13, A1 464, 1/1/1732.

BIBLIOGRAPHY

Belting, Natalia Marie, Kaskaskia under the French Regime, *Illinois Studies in the Social Sciences*, Reprint New Orleans, Polyanthos Press, 1975.

Brown, Margaret K., "Allons Cowboys!", *Journal of the Ill. State Historical Society*. LXXVI (1983):4.

Brown, Margaret K. and Lawrie Cena Dean, *The Village of Chartres in Colonial Illinois, 1720-1765*. New Orleans, Polyanthos Press, 1977.

Caldwell, Norman W., *The French in the Mississippi Valley, 1740-1750*. Urbana, University of Illinois Press, 1941.

Dean, Lawrie Cena and Margaret K. Brown. *The Kaskaskia Manuscripts 1714-1816: A Calendar of Civil Documents in Colonial Illinois*. Randolph County, Ill., microfilm, 1981. Cited as Kas. Mss.

Douville, Ramond and Jacques Casanova. *Daily Life in Early Canada*. New York, MacMillan Co., 1968.

Feiler, Seymour (ed.), *Travels in the Interior of North American 1751-1762*. Norman, University of Oklahoma Press, 1962.

Ford, Thomas. *A History of Illinois from its commencement as a State in 1818 to 1847*. Ann Arbor, Mich., University Microfilms,1968.

Gums, Bonnie L & Charles O. Witty. *A Glimpse of Village Life at Nouvelle Chartres*. Illinois Archeology 12,1 & 2, 2000.

Keefe, James F., "The Inventory of Fort de Chartres". *Muzzleloader*, Jan./Feb., 1992.

Louisiana Historical Quarterly. Various vols. and #s, 1917-1927. Baton Rouge, Louisiana. Cited as LHQ.

Mereness, Newton D. (ed.), *Travels in the American Colonies*. New York, MacMillan Co., 1916.

Morris, John L., *The French Regime in Illinois*. Ph.d. Thesis, Urbana, University of Illinois, 1928.

Paucton, *Métrologie ou Traité des Mesures, poids et monnoies...* Paris, Chez La Veuve Desaint, Libraire, 1780.

Pease, Theodore and Ernestine Jenison (eds), *Illinois on the Eve of the Seven Years War*, Collections of the Illinois State Historical Library, Vol. 29, Springfield, 1940.

Proulx, Gilles, *Between France and New France: Life Abroad the Tall Sailing Ships.* Louisiana State University Press, 1963.

Rowland, Dunbar and A.G. Sanders (eds.), *Mississippi Provincal Archives: French Dominion, 1704-1743.* 3 vols. Jackson, Miss., 1917-32. (cited as MPA)

Surrey, N.M. Miller, *The Commerce of Louisiana during the French Regime, 1699-1763.* Studies in History, Economics and Public Law, Vol.71:1, whole #167, New York, Columbia University, 1916.

Thwaites, R. G., *The French Regime in Wisconsin.* Coll. of the State Historical Society of Wisconsin, Vol. XVII, Madison, 1908.

--, Jesuit Relations and Allied Documents. 73 vols. Cleveland, Burrows Bros. Co., 1896-1901.

APPENDIX

The Complete Inventory of deTonty:

In the year 1737, on the 23rd day of June, we Alphonse de la Bussonniere, commandant in the Illinois, and the clerk of the court went to the house of the deceased Monsieur Antoine de Tonty at Fort de Chartres to put up for sale and auction the property of the said deceased, which was begun in the presence of Monsieur Joseph Gagnon, pastor of the said place and the undersigned witnesses, as follows. To wit:

One house situate at Fort de Chartres, 20 feet long by about 15 feet wide, of post-in-the-ground, covered with straw, in poor condition, built on a small lot bounding on Hebert Finette and on the other side on Becquet and generally whatever exists on the said lot, adjuged to Monsieur de Beausau, 192 livres.

Item, one cow adjudged to Baron, 82 livres.

Item, one said cow adjudged to Andre, 95 livres.

Item, two old broken guns, adjudged to the said Sieur de Louvier, 26 livres.

Item, a pair of andirons, a spit, the whole old, adjudged to Monsieur de Bausau, 42 livres.

Item, two candlesticks, a snuffer and tray of yellow copper and two poor pewter salt cellars, adjudged to Lebrun, 28 livres.

Continuation from the preceding [page]...465.

Item, one used half-beaver hat trimmed with silver adjudged to Legras, 40 livres.

Item, one regulation suit, one pair of (---), adjudged to LeComte, 30 livres.

Item, one old suit and vest of coffee-colored woolen broadcloth, adjudged to Monsieur Gagnon, 66 livres.

Item, one old suit and vest of gray woolen broadcloth, adjudged to Becquet the blacksmith, 28 livres.

Item, one old suit, vest and breeches of camleteen, the whole worn, adjudged to Thomas, 23 livres.

Item, one suit and two pairs of breeches in poor condition, adjudged to Becquet the blacksmith, 25 livres.

Item, four carrots of tobacco adjudged to Bacanet, 16 livres, ten sols.

Item, one mattress in poor condition, one small pillow, adjudged to Metivier, 26 livres.

Item, one coffer without a key, adjudged to La Chenain, 12 livres.

Item, one broken bottle case with ten flasks, of which five are broken, adjudged to Francois Becquet, 31 livres.

Continuation from the preceding [page] 762.#10.

Item, four used shirts, adjudged to Dominique, 71 livres.

Item, four other used shirts, adjudged to Landeau(?) 73 livres.

Item, one pair of old sheets, adjudged to St. Martin, 32 livres.

Item, one pair of used silk hose, a piece of cane, one small casket in poor condition, adjudged to Becquet the locksmith, 40 livres.

Item, two aunes of batiste to Madame St. Ange, 20 livres.

Item, 18 pewter plates and two platters to Madame St. Ange 46 livres.

Item, one yellow copper basin, one old skimmer, one carrot of tobacco to Madame St.Ange, 16 livres.

This was done and completed on the same day and year as the other parts and the monies to be received. We have charged Jerome Roussilliet who has promised to pay the deceased's debts known, and others which may arise and are truly owed, in order that later the remainder may be sent to the heirs, as much and as well as possible. At Fort de Chartres this said day the 23rd of June, 1737.

La Buissonniere; J. Gagnon, Priest.

(Kas. Mss. 37:6:23:1--translation by Lawrie Dean)
****

Inventory of Francois Blot.
(-) indicates damage to document.

The year 1740 the 30th day of January before noon, at the request of Thereise Boissait, widow of the deceased Francois Blot dit Charon living at St. Philippe of the great swamp in the Illinois, the parish of Fort de Chartres and in the presence of Sieur Gabriel Mettotte, deputy guardian of Francois, Thereise, Cecile, Agnes and Magdeline actual living heirs of the said deceased Francois Blot dit Charon their father. In the absence of Sieur Joseph Buchet attorney in the Illinois (-)[proceed] to the conservation of their rights upon the demand of the widow, to take up or renounce the community between her and the said deceased. I, Jerome Roussilliet, royal notary of Fort de Chartres in the Illinois undersigned proceeded to the inventory and description of all the goods, movable and immovable, found in the house where the said deceased has died. The said widow shows well and plainly by her authority that she has lent nothing nor hidden nor diverted anything of the whole. The evaulation and estimate is done by Sieurs Roch Pinguenet, Augustin Perrein dit Capucin, Jean Chauvin, Jean Gouin dit Champagne, and Pierre Butteau the father, inhabitants of Fort St. Philippe. The estimation was taken in the place and (-) the inventory was (-) in the following manner. The said Jean Chauvin, Pierre Butteau father and Jean Gouin dit Champagne have declared that they do not know how to write or sign following the ordinance. [Signatures] Pinguet, witness, Perint dit Capucin, witness, Jerome, notary.

First

A house of post-in-the-ground with a thatched roof, falling into ruin and (-) falling also into ruin, situated on a lot (-) arpent on the face by two in depth in the (-)[village] of St. Philippe of the Illinois bordering (-) to Germain and on the other to Sr. Chauvin, estimated 230 livres.

Item, land 3 arpents wide, the depth from the Mississippi to the hills, the whole located in the territory of St. Philippe in good condition (-) presently cultivated, bordering (-) and on the other (-) La Croix.

Item, an old black male slave named Pierrot "piece de Inde"[75] estimated 1200 livres.

Item, two oxen about 8 or 9 years, 300 livres.

Item, two oxen about 7 yrs. estimated 300 livres.

Item, two bulls about 3 years, estimated 200 livres.

Item, an old cow about 16 yrs. old, estimated 60 livres.

Item, a bull about 3 yrs, estimated 50 livres.

Item, a heifer of 7 or 8 months, estimated 20 livres.

Item, six large pigs, estimated each 30 livres, 180 livres.

---

[75] Piece d'Inde was "the standard value of a complete negro, that is 17 years old or over without bodily defects, or a negress without bodily defects, of 15 to 30 years, or three chldren of 8 to 10 years in age.", Natalia Marie Belting, "Kaskaskia under the French Regime", *Illinois Studies in the Social Sciences*, (reprint, New Orleans: Polyanthos Press, 1975), 38.

Item, eighteen small pigs at 10 livres each, 180 livres.

Item, fifty (-)[chickens?] altogether 50 livres.

Item, a (-) estimated 50 livres.

Item, an old grindstone, estimated 20 livres.

We stopped here and the continuation is delayed until tomorrow. The Srs. Jean Chauvin, Pierre Butteau father Jean Gouin dit Champagne and the said widow have declared they do not know how to write nor sign following the ordinance.

Perint dit Capucient, witness; Pinguenet, witness; Jerome, notary.

On the 30th of January 1740 continued the preparation of the inventory in the presence of those named above.

Item, five axes good and bad, estimated 25 livres.

Item, five spoon augurs for wheelworking, five gouges-two square and two round, nine augers, more large than small, two adzes, a round slater's hammer, a plane, an anvil, and a bucket hammer, all estimated 140 livres.

Item, a large cross cut saw and two saws, estimated 30 livres.

Item, an old gun with broken stock estimated 20 livres.

Item, four (-) estimated 10 livres.

Item, a cauldron (-) containing about six *pots* and another small (-), two pots pierced [colanders?], an old (-), estimated 21 livres.

Item, a (-) covered saucepan (-)of iron of two *pots*, estimated 25 livres.

Item, an old frying pan, estimated at 6 livres.

Item, eighteen old tin plates, 14 spoons also of tin, (-) nine old tin spoons, six forks (-)good, estimated 50 livres.

Item, two beds of (-), a poor pillow, two old buffalo robes, all estimated 80 livres.

Item, a feather bed, a straw mattress, two old robes and two old wool coverlets, all estimated 80 livres.

Item, a small walnut bed, estimated 10 livres.

Item, a walnut chest closing with a key, estimated 15 livres.

Item, fifty minots of wheat at 3 livres the minot, 150 livres.

Item, three cartloads of hay, 30 livres.

Debts of the Community

to the elder Heneaux, 24 minots of wheat

to Fr. Capucin, 10 livres.

to Petit Jean 10 livres 5 sols.

to Chauvin 6 livres.

The said inventory has been settled the said day and year below, and all goods mentioned in it, with the consent of all parties and the Sieurs (-) Metotte deputy guardian, have been delivered to the said widow who promised and promises to produce it when needed. Done at St. Philippe the day and year for the widow (-) Butteau the father, Jean Chauvin and Gabriel Mettote (-) dit Champagne have declared they do not know how to write (-) following the ordinance have signed. (-) witness; Pinguenet, witness; Jerome notary.

(Kas. Mss. 40:1:30:1--translation by the author)
****

Inventory of Michel LeCour

In the year one thousand seven hundred forty on the fourth day of June at two o'clock in the afternoon by virtue of the ordinance of Monsieur Louis Auguste De La Loere, Esquire, Sieur of Flancourt, Principal Scrivener of the Marine, subdelegate in the Illinois of Monsieur de Salmon, Commissioner of the Marine, Director in Louisiana, I, Jerome Roussilliet, Notary and Registrar at Fort de Chartres, have betaken myself to Cahokia to the house of the Sieur François Xavier Rolette, being assisted by the two witnesses undersigned in order to proceed to the inventory of the goods and effects which are in the home of the said Rolette belonging to the estate of the defunct LeCour, who died at Fort de Chartres at the home of the Sieur Roy on the first of the present month. After having removed the seal which I have ascertained to be whole and entire, having been applied by me on this morning and placed upon the door of a room and of a window of the house of the said Rolette where the said effects had been locked up and after having had the said Rolette swear under oath that he has neither diverted nor apprehended any item of the said goods and effects, we have begun the said inventory in the presence of the Sieur Jeacques Goufier, sergeant of the troops, commanding at the said Port (sic) of Cahokia and of the Sieur Jeacques Grignon, brother-in-law of the said defunct in the following manner:

FIRSTLY

There was found in a casket from which the seal has been removed an obligation made in Missouri in favor of Michel Le Court in the sum of twelve hundred eighty-four livres ten sous owed by Louis Levallé and Louis Tessier (?) upon which obligation has been endorsed the sum of four hundred sixty and eight livres in peltries, remaining due eight hundred sixteen livres...816#

Item, a note of Claude Le Deaut (?) for twenty livres ten sous...20# 10

Item, a note of Bellecour for the sum of ten livres and a dress dated the eighth May one thousand seven hundred thirty-nine...10#

Item, a note of Pichart in the sum of fifty three livres in peltries dated the twenty-first of February one thousand seven hundred thirty nine...53#

Item, a note of Chabot payable to the said defunct in the sum of forty seven livres dated the second of June one thousand seven hundred forty...47#

Item, a note of Claude Deaut(?) due to the said defunct in the sum of twenty-five livres dated the sixteenth October one thousand seven hundred thirty nine...25#

..... 971# 10

From the preceding [page].... 971# 10

Item, one note of the Sieur François Mercier due to the said defunct in the sum of thirty livres in peltry dated the fifth November one thousand seven hundred thirty nine and further a mirror at nine livres, together thirty-nine livres...39#

Item, a note of Louis Leduc due to the said defunct for a piece of printed calico fourteen aunes in length dated the twenty seventh May one thousand seven hundred thirty-eight.

Item, a note of one St. Onge in the sum of one hundred livres dated the twenty-sixth August one thousand seven hundred thirty-nine...100#

....1190# 10

Item, an account book belonging to Michel LeCour found in the said casket which has neither erasures nor strike-outs in which are amounts due by a number of individuals.

Item, a dressing case furnished with four razors, a stone, a leather and one pair of scissors, the whole in good condition.

Item, one dozen knives with wood handles and five woodcutter's knives, one dozen gun flints, one wad-extractor and one *batefeu*, two livres of powder and two aunes of *moleton*.[76]

Item, two new carbines and one long gun, used.

Item, four new shirts of *morlaix*[77] and a child's cap.

Item, one Indian slave about thirty years of age and her son, also an Indian about six or seven years of age.

Item, one large red copper kettle with holes in the bottom and ten sponges, small and large and one old covered kettle of red copper.

Item, in the said room where the seal was removed were found the following packs of peltry to wit, one said pack containing eight doe skins, turned and nine bear skins.

Item, one pack of buckskins weighing eighty livres...80#
Item, one pack of buckskins of eighty-two livres...82#
Item, one pack of buckskins of eighty-two livres...82#
Item, one pack of buckskins of sixty-seven livres...67#
Item, one said pack of buckskins weighing eighty-six livres...86#

....397#

From the preceding....397#
Item, one said pack of buckskins weighing seventy-nine livres...79#
Item, one said pack of buckskins weighing ninety-two livres...92#
Item, one said pack of buckskins weighing seventy-two livres...72#
Item, one said pack of buckskins weighing eighty-two livres...82#
Item, one said pack of buckskins weighing eighty-one livres...81#
Item, one said pack of buckskins weighing eighty-two livres...82#
Item, one said pack of buckskins weighing eighty livres...80#
Item, one said pack of buckskins weighing eighty-one livres...81#
Item, one said pack of buckskins weighing eighty-two livres...82#
Item, one said pack of buckskins weighing eighty-two livres...82#
Item, one said pack of buckskins weighing eighty-two livres...82#
Item, one said pack of buckskins weighing eighty-one livres...81#
Item, one said pack of buckskins weighing eighty-one livres...81#

---

[76]Guesses for these items are flintstone and wadding.

[77]This is a place name; there is also a fine gauze called *marli*.

Item, one said pack of buckskins weighing eighty-one livres...81#
Item, one said pack of buckskins weighing eighty-three livres...83#
Item, one said pack of buckskins weighing seventy-six livres...76#
Item, one said pack of buckskins weighing seventy-one livres...71#
Item, one said pack of buckskins weighing sixty-eight livres...68#
Item, one said pack of buckskins weighing sixty-seven livres...67#
Item, one said pack of buckskins weighing eighty-six livres...86#
Item, one said pack of buckskins weighing eighty-one livres...81#
Item, one said pack of buckskins weighing twenty-one livres...21#

The total of the said peltry/buckskin....2067
2063

Item, one pack of summer beaver weighing seventy-four livres...74#

Item, five large bear skins, five skins of large cubs and nine skins of small cubs, further ten large bear skin blankets/coverings, four cubskins, one green doeskin, one said of fawn.

Item, pack of seventeen bearskins.

There is owed by the estate of the said defunct the sum of three hundred livres to one Jean Batiste Soulart in wages, having been the hired man of the LeCourt, as stated in the acknowledgement of Joseph LeCour, which is in the possession of the said Soulart, payable at Montreal in peltry, made at Kaskaskia on the second April one thousand seven hundred forty.

There was found a bill for merchandise in the casket of the defunct by which, with a guarantee of interest, there is owed by the laid estate of the said LeCourt or by his brother who is at sea four thousand two hundred fifty-four livres seventeen sous three deniers to the Sieur Maugras which Joseph LeCourt borrowed, he who is at sea.

This was made and (includes) all the effects mentioned; the goods and papers included in the present inventory have been placed in the hands of the Sieur Jeacque Grignon, brother-in-law of the defunct Michel Le Court who has undertaken and undertakes by these presents and promises and binds himself to present them whenever there will be need and standing surety for heir or creditor has assigned his good, present and future with the exception of the two slaves who will be sold to pay the expenses in so far as funeral, surgeon and court. Made at Fort des Cahokias on this sixth June one thousand seven hundred forty. The said Sieur Jacque Grignon declares he does not how to write or to sign this instrument according to the ordinance and has made his usual mark.

Mark of the said Sieur Jeacque Grignon
Antoine Pothier, Scrivener; Chabot, witness; Jerome, Registrar; Sieur Jacques(?)

(Kas. Mss. 40:6:4:1--translated by Lawrie Dean)

Made in the USA
Lexington, KY
27 July 2016